POLITICAL
SCIENCE

THE FAITHFUL LEARNING SERIES

An Invitation to Academic Studies, Jay D. Green
Chemistry, Daniel R. Zuidema
Literature, Clifford W. Foreman
Music, Timothy H. Steele
Philosophy, James S. Spiegel
Political Science, Cale Horne
Sociology, Matthew S. Vos

JAY D. GREEN, SERIES EDITOR

POLITICAL SCIENCE

Cale Horne

PUBLISHING
P.O. BOX 817 • PHILLIPSBURG • NEW JERSEY 08865-0817

Scripture quotations are from the ESV® Bible (The Holy Bible, English Standard Version®), copyright © 2001 by Crossway, a publishing ministry of Good News Publishers. Used by permission. All rights reserved.

Italics within Scripture quotations indicate emphasis added.

The quotation on the back cover is from Hans J. Morgenthau, *Politics Among Nations: The Struggle for Power and Peace*, 5th ed. (New York: Alfred A. Knopf, 1973), 3.

Printed in the United States of America

Library of Congress Cataloging-in-Publication Data

Names: Horne, Cale D., 1978- author.
Title: Political science / Cale Horne.
Description: Phillipsburg : P&R Publishing, 2016. | Series: The faithful learning series
Identifiers: LCCN 2016000963| ISBN 9781596389014 (pbk.) | ISBN 9781596389021 (epub) | ISBN 9781596389038 (mobi)
Subjects: LCSH: Christianity and politics. | Political science--Philosophy.
Classification: LCC BR115.P7 H588 2016 | DDC 320.02/423--dc23
LC record available at http://lccn.loc.gov/2016000963

INTRODUCTION: WHAT POLITICAL SCIENCE IS . . . AND ISN'T

Casual conversations among strangers inevitably turn to work. When I find myself in such conversations with fellow Christians, once they discover that I am a political scientist I usually receive follow-up questions. I'm asked about the latest "breaking news" story coming out of the 24-hour news cycle, queried about whether I've read so-and-so's latest book or blog post on politics according to the Bible, or—most awkwardly—carefully probed to see whether my own political leanings are of the "right sort." I don't mind these kinds of discussions, and often enough they can be quite fun, but I do get the sense that the askers usually think that these things constitute what I *do* as a political scientist. But oftentimes my answers are a little disappointing: I don't follow the 24-hour news cycle all that closely, nor do I follow blogs, and only very rarely do I read popular books on the Bible and politics. At the end of the day, I'm not all that political in the everyday sense of the word.

I firmly believe that Christians can be concerned with political affairs from the local to the global. I say "can" rather than "should" or "must" because it seems presumptuous to think that our poorer brothers and sisters around the world, concerned with the full-time work of subsistence, are somehow less faithful as followers of Christ because of their ignorance of and disengagement from political affairs and their inability to articulate how political and other spheres of life pertain to their Christian faith. I mention this explicitly because the fact that the vast majority of Christians past and present have been unable to concern themselves with politics often seems lost on the champions of Christian political engagement. This should give us pause before we make any sort of cultural engagement a matter of basic duty. Rather, Christians who are in a position to be engaged in politics should feel the liberty to do so, for insights from political science can direct us toward productive avenues for faithful engagement as well as help us to avoid the all too frequent conflation of faithful engagement with faith-distorting entanglement. As Jay Green, the editor of this series on faithful learning, suggests, I argue that serious engagement with the academic study of politics may indeed "cultivate and nourish our faith in Christ" when we choose to enter the arena of government and politics.

Despite American Christianity's enduring interest in the political world—including perennial debates over whether, how, and why believers should engage in the contemporary political discourse—very few among us have a sense of how the academic study of politics may contribute to or even clarify these debates. In fact, I would argue that very few Christians have even a general grasp of what the academic study of politics (most often termed "political science") *is*, though many may presume to know. In keeping with the theme of the Faithful Learning series, I outline in this booklet the broad contours of the discipline, present a Christian framework for approaching political science rooted in antithesis and common grace, and illustrate the potential for faithful learning in and through the study of politics as an academic discipline.

Simply defined, political science is an empirically based, theoretically driven social science addressing human endeavors of a political nature. Broadly speaking, the discipline seeks to understand the patterns of cooperation and conflict among people and groups—the conditions under which individuals or groups of individuals with divergent interests will (or will fail to) cooperate in order to achieve common goals.[1] In the words of famed political scientist Harold Lasswell, "The study of politics is the study of influence and the influential," or, as the title of the now-classic book from which this quotation is drawn suggests, political science is the study of "who gets what, when, how."[2] The answers to these core disciplinary questions, and the policy efforts designed to reinforce or alter the answers to these questions, have profound implications for the world we inhabit.

Three of the discipline's four subfields address areas of substantive concern: in the United States (American government), within states generally (comparative politics), and between states (international relations). The fourth subfield, political theory, takes up conceptual (and sometimes normative) concerns and undergirds the other three.[3] Like other social sciences, political science is motivated by *empirical puzzles*—things we observe in the political world that don't make sense in an easy or obvious way. For example, a comparativist (that is, a specialist in comparative politics who compares the inputs and outputs of different political systems) might seek to explain why democracy succeeds in one country but flounders in a similar country. Or an international-relations scholar may wonder why democratic states rarely, if ever, seem to go to war with one another, though they tend to be more war prone than their nondemocratic neighbors. The explanations to these

---

1. This is not to suggest that cooperation is intrinsically or normatively good. Individuals might cooperate, for example, to instigate and carry out genocide. Rather, cooperation should be thought of as the means by which people who possess different wants and goals come together to get more of whatever good they would otherwise have.

2. Harold D. Lasswell, *Politics: Who Gets What, When, How* (New York: McGraw-Hill, 1936), 295.

3. Some political scientists regard research methods as a fifth, distinct subfield.

puzzles adopted by political elites and the public at large can seriously impact government policies, economies, and societies—and, ultimately, communities, families and individuals. Getting it right matters.

As I mentioned above, political science as a discipline is theoretically driven and empirically based. Theories in the social sciences are stories we tell about the world to explain the often puzzling things we observe in the world. From a given theory we derive hypotheses—empirically testable propositions of the theory that allow us to know whether this explanation is wrong.[4] We test hypotheses *empirically*—that is, using information we observe about the world (data) and specific tools to gather and manipulate data for hypothesis testing (research methods). Data and the methods used to draw inferences from these data may be *qualitative* (e.g., single case studies, comparative case studies, historical process-tracing, counterfactual analysis) or *quantitative* (statistical analysis, computational network analysis, simulation), and frequently research is comprised of some combination of the two—the line between qualitative and quantitative research is often blurry. Significantly, both qualitative and quantitative methods apply the same logic of empirical inquiry as summarized above.[5] Choices

4. We can never demonstrate that a hypothesis is "right," but only whether it is "wrong" or "not wrong." This is not because of a commitment to some sort of pop-postmodernism in which we can never know truth, but because the social sciences, like all empirically oriented disciplines, must operate according to the logic of empirical inquiry. Hypothesis testing can only tell us that a given explanation is wrong/not wrong (never right) because an infinite number of other explanations always go untested. Testing one or several of what seem to be the most likely explanations does not provide enough information to rule out other, untested explanations. The logic of hypothesis testing is related to the principle of *falsifiability*: hypotheses must be constructed in such a way that we can know by testing the hypothesis whether or not the explanation proposed is wrong.

5. Gary King, Robert O. Keohane, and Sidney Verba, *Designing Social Inquiry: Scientific Inference in Qualitative Research* (Princeton: Princeton University Press, 1994).

about methods, then, depend on what is appropriate given the research question in view.

This approach to understanding politics is far removed from the experience of most Christians. Many of us think of politics in terms of daily headlines, newsfeeds, sound bites, and talking heads. The issues are ever changing and are rarely explained in terms of underlying institutional processes, the psychological dynamics of decision making, or long-term historical trends. We may also regard politics as an ideological battleground—a sphere to be reclaimed (or avoided) and rebuilt (or abandoned) according to a (usually vague) biblical template. Regardless of one's theology or place on the ideological spectrum, there is a baptized political movement to match, ranging from the theonomic reconstructionist and Christian America movements on the political right to the various strains of transformationalism and liberation theology on the left.

Despite their radical differences, all such movements have at least two features in common. First, adherents tend to value the political interpretations of their anointed leaders over the careful study of professional academics, which is deemed irrelevant at best. Second, and more fundamentally, these movements reflect a common discomfort with just how little the Bible really says about politics.[6] Rather than revealing the larger story of the redemption of God's

6. The contemporary obsession with prooftexting our way through all things political seems contrary to the simplest statements of Reformed orthodoxy: "Q: What do the Scriptures principally teach? A: The Scriptures principally teach, what man is to believe concerning God, and what duty God requires of man" (Westminster Confession of Faith [WCF] Larger Catechism [LC], Q&A #5). A recent and highly popular example of what I would regard as a kind of discomfort with how little the Bible says about politics is Wayne Grudem's *Politics—According to the Bible: A Comprehensive Resource for Understanding Modern Political Issues in Light of Scripture* (Grand Rapids: Zondervan, 2010). Another example, from another part of the political spectrum, is the work of Jim Wallis, beginning with his *Agenda for Biblical People* (New York: Harper & Row, 1976).

people, the Scriptures become a blueprint for political (in)action—something for which they were never intended. Indeed, to reinterpret the Scriptures to reinforce one's political agenda is not merely exegetically unsound, it is sacrilegious. How dare we "spin" the Word of God to advance our political agendas!

As an alternative, I propose that we employ the historic Christian framework of antithesis and common grace to the academic disciplines, including the study of politics. By taking seriously both antithesis and common grace, Christians have a framework not only for *critiquing* the discipline but also for conscientiously *embracing* many of its premises, methods, theories, and findings. To the extent that the discipline operates within the bounds of common grace, it has a role in the unfolding of God's providential order and should be embraced by Christians interested in faithful learning. The result, I believe, is an enriched understanding of both the academic study of politics and the relationship of this study to our faith.

In the final analysis, the academic disciplines (though fallen and flawed) are expressions of human learning graciously granted by God to sustain his appointed order until that final day. If we understand the essence of history as the *unfolding revelation* of the redemption of God's people, the disciplines—even when wielded by the pagan—are instruments for the sustenance of creation, and thus for *our* own sustenance, as we move through creation to consummation. Like the rain that falls on the just and the unjust alike, the disciplines are good gifts from God. When the disciplines are properly understood through the framework of antithesis and common grace, believers individually and the church corporately do not need to be shielded from them, but can be blessed by them.

A CHRISTIAN FRAMEWORK FOR APPROACHING POLITICAL SCIENCE

I do not wish to restate the argument for faithful learning that has been so eloquently outlined by Jay Green in the opening volume of this series. However, it seems appropriate to build on Green's thesis in a way specific to my own discipline and to reiterate one or two of his own points along the way. I share Green's frustration with the project of Christian scholarship, in which the tendency to think philosophically and theologically about academic disciplines often gives short shrift to disciplinary content and contributions. The admonitions and formulae coming from many corners—ranging from "transformation/redemption" of creation/culture to "faithful presence" in it—tend to be vague and unconcerned with the nuts and bolts of scholarship, Christian or otherwise. Others have brought the very project of Christian scholarship into question, opting for a "two kingdoms" dualism, whereby natural law guides believer and unbeliever alike in the neutral realm of the academy.[7] I reach back to what I believe is a position inherent in and flowing out of historic, Reformed orthodoxy—the paradigm of antithesis and common grace—and argue that *faithful learning is a direct and necessary consequence of this understanding of the world and the believer's place in it.*

---

7. Generally speaking, proponents of the two-kingdoms perspective argue for the existence of a civil/common kingdom and a spiritual/redemptive kingdom (while largely failing to articulate a third, antithetical kingdom consisting of those things given over to Satan [i.e., Gen. 3:15]). The assumption, then, is that the common kingdom—as its name suggests—is neutral territory where the identity and presuppositions of its participants (who are themselves members of either God's redemptive kingdom or the Satanic one—either the line of Seth or the line of Cain) have no bearing. See David VanDrunen, *Natural Law and the Two Kingdoms: A Study in the Development of Reformed Social Thought* (Grand Rapids: Eerdmans, 2010).

Antithesis and Common Grace

What do I mean by *antithesis* and *common grace*?[8] Antithesis refers to the innate and fundamental difference and separateness of God and his redeemed people (whom we call the church, in both its Old and New Testament manifestations) from all who have rebelled against God and are committed to destruction, represented by Satan. This state of affairs dates to Satan's fall and the subsequent fall of man depicted in Genesis 3. Antithesis suggests that there is no middle ground or neutral territory between a state of covenant fellowship with God and a state of rebellion against him, which is fellowship with Satan. From the fall onward, all humanity is divided into these two mutually exclusive lines—the line of Seth and the line of Cain—and the unfolding history of redemption is characterized by enmity between them, building toward the climactic end when Christ "shall bruise [Satan's] head" (Gen. 3:15). Antithesis, then, is the defining characteristic of all reality and the appropriate lens through which the believer begins to interpret the world.

But, because the graciousness of God extends even to our earthly existence, antithesis is not where our interpretation of the world needs to end! Despite his state of enmity with

8. The themes addressed here are developed at length in Cornelius Van Til's collection of essays on the subject; see Cornelius Van Til, *Common Grace and the Gospel*, 2nd ed. (Phillipsburg, NJ: P&R Publishing, 2015). Of course any discussion of Reformed conceptions of common grace owe an inestimable debt to Abraham Kuyper, who authored a three-volume series on the subject; see *De Gemeene Gratie*, 3 vols. (Amsterdam: Höveker & Wormser, 1902–04). Translated excerpts of this series can be found in James D. Bratt, ed., *Abraham Kuyper: A Centennial Reader* (Grand Rapids: Eerdmans, 1998), 165–204. Kuyper's work on common grace with respect to science and the arts—portions of which were accidentally omitted from *De Gemeene Gratie*—has recently been translated as a standalone volume: Abraham Kuyper, *Wisdom and Wonder: Common Grace in Science and Art*, trans. Nelson D. Kloosterman (Grand Rapids: Christian's Library Press, 2011). The entirety of *De Gemeene Gratie* is presently being translated into English for the first time through a joint project of the Acton Institute and Kuyper College.

those who belong to Satan, God "makes his sun rise on the evil and on the good, and sends rain on the just and on the unjust" (Matt. 5:45). That is, a tangible expression of God's grace to all people is restraining the outward, creational effects of the fall upon humanity. And this is just the beginning. God also restrains the ontological effects of the fall *within* human beings. In his classic formulation, Abraham Kuyper describes how common grace dispensed to the pagan is manifested in two ways. In the negative sense, common grace restrains the unbeliever's depravity, so that no one is as evil as they might be. Yet in the positive sense, it allows the unbeliever—even apart from regeneration through special grace—the capability of doing good in a limited way as a (corrupted) image-bearer of God.[9] Kuyper also speaks of these two sides of common grace as *constant* (the negative sense) and *progressive* (the positive sense). By "progressive" he seems to have in mind all humanity (regenerate and unregenerate) as "colaborers" with God in history.[10] In other words, common grace empowers the unbeliever to participate in the historical unfolding of God's providential order—an idea that deserves further exploration.[11]

Common grace also has epistemological dimensions—that is, implications for how unbelievers can know something of the created order and participate in its unfolding despite their lack of submission to the Creator.[12] The pagan and the believer alike can know that 2 + 2 = 4, though only the

9. Van Til, *Common Grace*, 15. For an overview of the Reformed positions on common grace, see William D. Dennison, "Van Til and Common Grace," *Mid-America Journal of Theology* 9, no. 2 (Fall 1993): 225–47.

10. Van Til, *Common Grace*, 17. See also WCF 16:7.

11. See Abraham Kuyper, "Common Grace," in Bratt, *Centennial Reader*, 174–76.

12. There are, of course, other dimensions of common grace, including the (believing and unbelieving) human capacity for self-awareness and the awareness of and interaction with one's environment, though space does not permit a discussion of these things here.

believer acknowledges that this fact is *created*, that even the most fundamental principles of mathematics and logic exist because God says they exist. The pagan, by contrast, regards $2 + 2 = 4$ as an autonomous fact surmised by reason alone. In this sense, only the believer really *knows* that $2 + 2 = 4$ in the most meaningful sense, because he knows the author of this fact and understands that this and other facts do not exist in isolation; they are parts of the fabric of a created and unfolding order. Whereas the unbeliever may regard $2 + 2 = 4$ as self-evident, it is actually evident (or knowable) only because God makes it so and reveals it as such. This is common grace. Apart from this dimension of common grace working in the minds of believers and unbelievers, human existence would be untenable, much as it would be in the absence of sun and rain. And, like the universal blessing of sun and rain, the epistemological dimension and other dimensions of common grace are not ends in themselves but are God's implements for bringing all things to completion in him. The epistemological dimension of common grace should also give us some confidence in our ability to engage enthusiastically with the academic disciplines, even when those disciplines' leading voices are unbelievers who can't *really* know (in a biblically self-conscious manner) that $2 + 2 = 4$!

Van Til's Transcendental Critique

Such enthusiastic engagement, however, should not be confused with an uncritical embrace of the thought and work of unbelieving academics. Indeed, understanding antithesis and common grace is the basis for what Reformed apologist Cornelius Van Til called the *transcendental critique* of human knowledge.[13] Van Til believed that the starting point

13. For a very gentle introduction to Van Til's transcendental critique, see William D. Dennison, "Van Til's Critique of Human Thought," *New Horizons*, October 2004, 9–10. For insightful introductions to Van Til generally, see Greg

for Christian scholarship, and indeed for all knowledge, is the self-attesting Christ of Scripture.[14] For the Christian, all knowledge—knowledge of the self, others, and the world—issues from this starting point: namely, the knowledge of God as he has revealed himself. Indeed, all humans possess a knowledge of God and are accountable for it, though some have suppressed this truth in unrighteousness (Romans 1:18–32).

Interacting with, critiquing, and correcting thinking—both our own and that of the broader world—is at the very center of the transcendental critique and its distinctly Christian approach to scholarship. In his transcendental critique, Van Til is indicating a method for uncovering the presuppositions of any human principle or system of thought. In the scholarly world, this takes the form of examining and disclosing the structures of human thought to discover the root beliefs about the world and ultimately the Archimedean point (i.e., vantage point) governing it all. For the Christian, it is in the Archimedean point of Jesus' self-attestation—seen in the gospel throughout Scripture—that the transcendental critique finds its basis. Indeed, the Christian must participate self-consciously in the worldview of Scripture in order to critique the world and himself. "Inwardly," Greg Bahnsen describes it, "Van Til's presuppositional approach calls for self-examination by Christian scholars and apologists to see if their own theories of knowledge have been self-consciously developed in subordination to the word of God which they wish to vindicate or apply."[15]

L. Bahnsen, *Van Til's Apologetic: Readings and Analysis* (Phillipsburg, NJ: P&R Publishing, 1998), 1–26; and William Edgar and K. Scott Oliphint, eds., *Christian Apologetics Past and Present: A Primary Source Reader*, vol. 2, *From 1500* (Wheaton, IL: Crossway, 2011), 453–56.

14. William D. Dennison, "The Christian Academy: Antithesis, Common Grace, and Plato's View of the Soul," *Journal of the Evangelical Theological Society* 54, no. 1 (March 2011): 114.

15. Bahnsen, *Van Til's Apologetic*, 13.

The *true* knowledge made accessible through the Archimedean point of Christ, which forms the basis of Christian scholarship, is inseparable from the gospel message. All things (including, but not limited to, the world of human experience and scholarship) are subject to the authority of Christ and hold together in him (John 1:3; Col. 1:16–17), and it is to the self-attesting Christ—over and against the world—that we are called to always be ready to make a humble defense (1 Peter 3:15). *Faith and learning*—identified in Christ and in a pursuit of knowledge through Christ—are inextricably bound together in the project of Christian scholarship.

Faithful learning—joyful participation in the fruits of scholarly life for the good of the church—is a natural consequence and the necessary end of the understanding of antithesis and common grace presented here. Even laboring under the effects of the fall, believers and unbelievers alike can participate in the unfolding of God's providential plan for the creation. Because academic disciplines at their best are directed (knowingly or unknowingly) toward that unfolding, the church corporately and believers individually should actively look to the disciplinary insights gleaned by common grace in order to keep from error and better glorify God. And, because common grace must always be preceded by antithesis (that is, framed by transcendental critique) as we seek to understand the world, Christian scholars, colleges, and schools, as well as informed elders, deacons, and laity in the church, all have a part to play.

Application to Political Science

A few remarks are in order about how the antithesis–common grace framework, which leads to faithful learning, can be applied to my discipline, political science. I will limit my illustration of the antithesis–common grace framework here to a discussion of empirical theory, though we could just as well apply this framework to research questions, issues of data selection, research methods, or the scientific method itself. I opt to focus on theory because theoretical choices are strongly connected to, and determinative of, the other elements of empirical inquiry.

Empirical theory—our explanations of the observable world—necessarily omits some facts while giving serious explanatory weight to others.[16] Such omissions are good things insofar as we want theories to be parsimonious (think "Occam's razor"—the notion that, all else equal, the simplest explanation is the best one). However, the fact that theory is a choice of explanation about how the world does (and does not) work should also highlight for us theory's importance to empirical inquiry. Whether God is acknowledged or not, a theory that best conforms to special revelation will be a better describer and predictor of the world we actually observe. This is obvious when stated a little differently: general revelation (God's revelation of himself to all people, which the academic disciplines have a part in interpreting) will be compatible with special revelation (Scripture: God's redemptive self-revelation to his covenant people). Since God is the author of both "books," though they do not say the same thing, they certainly will not contradict one another. So, while special revelation is not *sufficient* for good theory building, good theory will be *consistent* with special revelation insofar as it is applicable.

In the social sciences, the applicability of special revelation to theory building can be profound inasmuch as the social sciences are concerned with patterns of human

16. I am limiting my discussion here to empirical theory (intended to explain the way the world is) while omitting normative theory (intended to explain the way the world ought to be), which is more appropriately the province of philosophy rather than social science.

behavior. In my mind, the greatest common-grace insight built into the social sciences is the overarching assumption that human nature *exists*—that there is such a thing—and that it is, in some sense, knowable. Given the assumption that there is such a thing as human nature, it becomes reasonable to search for patterns in human behavior and to make generalizations about this behavior while positing explanations for it. Describing and predicting human behavior, based on the assumption that humans possess a generalizable nature attributable to humankind as a whole, is what the social sciences are all about.[17]

That said, an appeal to the antithesis must frame the social sciences' fundamental, common-grace insight regarding human nature. We quickly find that, while affirming the existence of human nature, the social sciences as a whole are agnostic or else divided about the actual content of that nature, which is where theory comes into play and where special revelation can inform theory building. Indeed, God's special revelation is anything but agnostic on the subject of human nature. From Scripture we learn that, due to original sin imputed from the fall, human nature is wholly corrupt and spiritually dead. The Westminster Confession of Faith echoes this theme in strident terms, stating, "From this original corruption . . . we are utterly indisposed, disabled, and made opposite to all good, and wholly inclined to all evil" (WCF 6:4). The effects of this sinful nature on

17. There are some theoretical schools in the social sciences that take exception to the claim of a generalizable human nature. In political science, these exceptions include some cultural theories (where assumed identities, not innate natures, are used to explain human behavior) as well as some constructivist theories (where humans' shared "constructions" of meaning, such as a belief in the anarchic nature of the international system, frame their responses to experience). Of course not all cultural and constructivist theories fit this criticism easily, and many cultural and constructivist theorists have facilitated important advances in the discipline.

human behavior are immense: "The [inward] punishments of sin in this world, are . . . as blindness of mind, a reprobate sense, strong delusions, hardness of heart, horror of conscience, and vile affections" (LC #28). Original sin has profound implications for how human beings perceive and respond to the world around them, and it consequently has profound implications for thinking about theories intended to describe, explain, and predict human behavior.

When the unbelieving political scientist is acting less like his true self (depraved) and more like an image-bearer of God due to the active presence of common grace in his life, his thinking about theory will come closer to explaining the way things really are.[18] In terms of our example of assumptions about human nature, this means building theory that incorporates rather than denies the human capacity for evil. A tangible example of this sort of excellent theory building on the part of unbelievers can be seen in the realist school of international relations that developed in the aftermath of the Second World War. This school of thought was led largely by a group of European Jewish scholars who fled or survived the Holocaust and migrated to the United States. This small band of intellectuals was under no illusions about the depravity of human nature and, led by the towering figure of Hans Morgenthau, built a theory of relations between states based upon this core assumption.

In his opus, *Politics Among Nations*—possibly the most important book ever written on international politics— Morgenthau from the beginning regards human nature as central to the realist project: "Political realism believes that

---

18. To be explicit, not every finding from academia constitutes common grace—far from it. Common grace is really common grace only insofar as it is compatible with biblical revelation. Otherwise the language of common grace simply becomes a convenient means for baptizing secular thought.

politics, like society in general, is governed by objective laws that have their roots in human nature. . . . The operation of these laws being impervious to our preferences, men will challenge them only at the risk of failure."[19] He goes on to describe this nature as "interest defined in terms of power," where interest is a universally valid, objective category "unaffected by the circumstances of time and place," and where power "may comprise anything that establishes and maintains the control of man over man."[20]

Realism has serious implications for understanding the behavior of states in the international system. States go to war when it is in their interest to do so, given the perception of likely benefits and costs, and regardless of considerations that we might regard as ethical. Thus states will be suspicious of one another and will maintain a constant state of readiness for war, since they may at times be incentivized to mask their own specific interests and capabilities. Because self-interest and uncertainty pervade the international system, a state cannot readily rely on other states to come to its aid when threatened by another; even legally binding military alliances should be seen as more or less temporary and bendable alignments of mutual interest rather than rock-solid commitments to mutual defense based on a common culture or moral principles. In fact, states that fail to abide by the interest-based, power-driven state of affairs that defines international politics risk dropping out of the system altogether. The realist message to states, in a nutshell, is this: "Ignore human nature at your own peril."

By contrast, the believing political scientist who is acting less like his true self (regenerate) will be guided by

---

19. Hans J. Morgenthau, *Politics Among Nations: The Struggle for Power and Peace*, 5th ed. (New York: Alfred A. Knopf, 1973), 4.
20. Ibid., 5, 8–9.

theoretical explanations that are less in touch with the ways things really are. Continuing with the example of human nature and international politics, we might consider the case of Woodrow Wilson—a dynamic Princeton political scientist who eventually became president of the university, the twenty-eighth president of the United States, and a devout Presbyterian!—whose unfortunate approach to foreign policy in the aftermath of World War I set the stage for the ascent of political realism in the following generation.

Woodrow Wilson came to epitomize the liberal, or *idealist*, school of international relations (against which the reactionary term *realism* was coined). Embodied in his vision for the League of Nations, Wilson was a proponent of the political philosophy articulated by Immanuel Kant (1724–1804), who held that "perpetual peace" among nations was both a moral imperative and a rational possibility. Kant was in turn building on the thought of Hugo Grotius (1583–1645), who held that reason dictates that law based on a golden-rule dynamic should guide not only legal relations among individuals, but legal relations among states as well. States should agree to restrain their own behavior, operating in an "international society" governed by shared norms.

Building on Grotius, Kant held that such an international society was possible in the presence of three elements, known as the "Kantian Triangle." *Republicanism* (democracy) is the first leg: Kant believed that wars would be less likely to start if governments were elected by those who would do the fighting and dying. Both republicanism and peace would be reinforced by Kant's second leg, *universal hospitality*— what we would call free trade—in which the unencumbered movement of goods and services is broadly beneficial to the inhabitants of states and mutually beneficial across states.

Finally, and critically, Kant's world of commerce-bound republics is held together and expanded under the rubric of a *cosmopolitan constitution* (Grotius's international law), which recognizes and protects these networks of exchange and the republics across which they operate.[21]

In the Kantian framework, states are ultimately able to subjugate their differences via a shared commitment to republicanism, which forms the basis for economic and security cooperation among them. Woodrow Wilson sought to realize Kant's vision in the League of Nations, an assembly of democracies bound together by shared ideals and committed to a system of *collective security* on this basis. Collective security refers to the idea that states can codify their defensive military commitments to one another through international law and can rely on these commitments— instead of on their own capacity for self-defense and on the ability to balance power with power—in the face of external aggression. Such a system would work well, Morgenthau said, except that "those nations must be willing to subordinate their conflicting political interests to the common good defined in terms of the collective defense of all member states."[22] His skepticism about the possibilities for subordinating human nature to cooperation finds credence in actual state behavior, as was tragically borne

21. Immanuel Kant, *Perpetual Peace*, trans. and ed. Lewis White Beck (1795; repr., Indianapolis: Bobbs-Merrill, 1957).

22. Morgenthau, *Politics Among Nations*, 408. Additionally, two other conditions must be satisfied for collective-security arrangements to hold: (1) the parties to the agreement must at all times maintain adequate force to overwhelm and thereby deter any potential aggressor; and (2) the parties must share the same idea of security that they are agreeing to defend (ibid.). Also, at least one other condition could be added to Morgenthau's list: the collective-security arrangement must be seen as *credible*—i.e., parties to the contract will fulfill their obligations under it—both in the eyes of its members as well as those of potential challengers. This is the heart of the collective-action problem intrinsic to all such associations.

out by the Russo-Polish War (1921), the Franco-Belgian invasion of the Ruhr (1923), the Chaco War between Bolivia and Paraguay (1932), the Second Italian-Abyssinian War (1935), the Second Sino-Japanese War (1937), the German remilitarization of the Rhineland (1936) and occupation of the Sudetenland and *Anschluss* with Austria (1938), the Soviet invasion of Finland (1939), and the German occupation of Czechoslovakia and invasion of Poland (1939) leading to World War II—all of which fell under League jurisdiction. Wilsonian idealism is not a basis for international relations.

Clearly, applying the transcendental critique to the core disciplinary concern of theory building is not just a critique in the simple sense. We as Christian scholars are not on a slash-and-burn mission to learn about the assumptions and practices of a scholarly discipline only to tear it down with a "we-know-better" sense of righteous indignation. As John Frame states it, "To Van Til, 'antithesis' is not only a means of criticizing others; it is also a key to the very formulation of Christian truth. Van Til [shows] that Christian theology is a *system* of truth, that its elements are so profoundly interrelated that to deny one doctrine is implicitly to deny the whole."[23]

With antithesis in view, we approach academic disciplines with gratitude as *God's good and purposeful gifts*, and, understanding ourselves as members of Christ's body who are caught up in the eschatological drama of revelation history, we give thanks that we can participate in that unfolding through our engagement with these things. By participating in academia and other human institutions, and by virtue of God's common grace, we are participants in the unfolding of the two lines of humanity—Cain and

---

23. John M. Frame, "Van Til on Antithesis," *Westminster Theological Journal* 57, no. 1 (Spring 1995): 82.

Seth—that are moving in wholly *uncommon* (antithetical) directions. If we remain mindful that *un*faithful learning is a real possibility when we engage with academic disciplines, faithful learning makes us more like the place we are going. The following section gives two examples—one based in economic theory and the other in psychological theory—of research agendas that I consider to be among the best instances of faithful learning in political science today.

FAITHFUL LEARNING ILLUSTRATED: THE LOGIC OF POWER AND ATTITUDES TOWARD RISK

Selectorate Theory

Unlike Morgenthau's earlier (some would say "pre-theoretical") formulation, in latter renditions of realist theory the state becomes the only meaningful unit of analysis. By "unit of analysis" I mean the type of actor to which a hypothesis applies (individuals, groups, institutions, and so on). For example, consider the hypothesis, "In a majority-rule electoral system, successful candidates in a general election will tend to align themselves closer to the preferences of most voters, in contrast with their primary-election stances."[24] Here the unit of analysis is the shift in candidate positions from primary to general elections. Or consider this: "Democracies are less likely to initiate a war than non-democracies." Here the unit of analysis is the

---

24. We could also rework this hypothesis to consider the voter as the unit of analysis. The example is derived from Duncan Black's famous "median voter theorem," one of the most widely used and fundamental arguments in rationalist explanations of democratic elections and decision making. In short, the winner of an election in a majority-rule system is the "equilibrium candidate," meaning the one closest to the preferences of the most voters, such that these voters have no incentive to change their votes and the candidate has no incentive to change positions (see Duncan Black, "On the Rationale of Group Decision-making," *Journal of Political Economy* 56, no. 1 [February 1948]: 23–34).

state, requiring us to design a test to determine whether democratic states are more, less, or equally as war-prone as their non-democratic counterparts.

Realism's emphasis on the state makes sense in many ways. Political realists have always been concerned with interstate conflict, which involves states fighting with or against other states, as well as with the state-centered reasons for conflict, such as the balance of power. However, by adopting the state as its exclusive unit of analysis, realism could not appreciate important causal variables below the level of the state (domestic politics, institutions, technology) or above the level of the state (the distribution of power, geography, climate). More fundamentally, many political scientists began to argue that it isn't states that make decisions; only people make decisions. Consequently they began to look below the level of the state, to the individuals that make up states—as well as the preferences, roles, institutions, and capabilities that characterize each of those individuals, and the interactions among them—in order to understand the behavior that is commonly attributed to the state collectively.

Selectorate theory is one very specific, and particularly fruitful, outworking of this critique of realism. Originating in the 1990s, selectorate theory begins with one very simple, powerful assumption: leaders of states want to keep it that way. That is to say, all else equal, the foremost goal of any leader is to survive in office. Leaders seek to achieve this goal by appealing to the interests of a *winning coalition*: the individual supporters drawn from the pool of all possible supporters (*the selectorate*) whose backing is required for the leader to retain office.[25]

25. Fortunately, two of the originators of selectorate theory have summarized many of the theory's major implications in an insightful and entertaining book intended for a popular audience: Bruce Bueno de Mesquita and Alastair Smith, *The*

Regardless of what is good for the citizens of a country as a whole or what makes sense according to realism's logic of interest-based state behavior, leaders who wish to remain leaders will make sure that their winning coalitions are satisfied *above all other concerns.* According to this logic—the logic of leadership survival—leaders will want their coalitions to be as small as possible. The fewer people they need to satisfy in order to retain power, the easier the coalition will be to manage. Very small coalitions (as in dictatorships) can be paid off with private, divisible goods (i.e., goods that can be provided to some while withheld from others), while larger coalitions (as in democracies) can be rewarded with public goods (i.e., goods that benefit a non-excludable group, such as improved roads to reward areas comprised of mostly loyal constituents).

The need to "pay off" coalition members—in both democracies and non-democracies—has other implications for leader behavior. For example, a leader's ability to provide payoffs is a function of that leader's control of state resources. This is why democratic systems are, on average, so much less corrupt and better managed than non-democracies: in a democracy, the leader's control of the purse strings is severely (and intentionally) curtailed, meaning that a much broader range of interests must be satisfied when it comes to resource allocation. This doesn't mean that policymaking is perfect, but we don't generally see democratically elected leaders spending state funds on personal palaces, yachts, and the like for themselves and their cronies, which is a common trait of non-democratic, small-coalition systems. Instead, the currency of democratic

---

Dictator's Handbook: Why Bad Behavior Is Almost Always Good Politics (New York: PublicAffairs, 2011). Bibliographic references to much of the academic literature on selectorate theory can be found in *The Dictator's Handbook.*

leaders is *policy*: democratic coalitions reward policy success and punish policy failure.[26]

A related rule of political survival drawn from selectorate theory is, "Don't take money out of your supporters' pockets to make the people's lives better."[27] This isn't to say that all politicians are power-crazed and maniacal. Many political leaders have noble intentions and wish to serve their constituents well according to the rule of law. The point here from selectorate theory is that noble intentions don't necessarily matter: "If you're good to the people at the expense of your coalition, it won't be long until your 'friends' will be gunning for you."[28] In other words, the logic of selectorate theory is just that: *logic*. And leaders who consistently fail to behave according to this logic won't remain leaders for long. The paradox of political leadership, then, is that what constitutes good policy for the people you wish to lead isn't necessarily good policy for retaining the leadership role needed to make policy.

Though a relatively new idea, selectorate theory has already been applied across a number of areas of political inquiry: leadership survival and the domestic-political consequences of interstate wars,[29] military interventions,[30] sanctions against foreign governments,[31] and foreign aid,[32] to

26. Ibid., 17–20.

27. Ibid., 18.

28. Ibid.

29. Bruce Bueno de Mesquita and Randolph M. Siverson, "War and the Survival of Political Leaders: A Comparative Study of Regime Types and Political Accountability," *The American Political Science Review* 89, no. 4 (December 1995): 841–55. See also Bruce Bueno de Mesquita, Randolph M. Siverson, and Gary Woller, "War and the Fate of Regimes: A Comparative Analysis," *The American Political Science Review* 86, no. 3 (September 1992): 638–46.

30. Bruce Bueno de Mesquita and George W. Downs, "Intervention and Democracy," *International Organization* 60, no. 3 (Summer 2006): 627–49.

31. Fiona McGillivray and Alastair Smith, *Punishing the Prince: A Theory of Interstate Relations, Political Institutions, and Leader Change* (Princeton: Princeton University Press, 2008).

32. Bruce Bueno de Mesquita and Alastair Smith, "A Political Economy of

name a few; plus as a corrective to simplistic narratives about culture and race.[33] Far from an abstract academic tool, selectorate theory has been applied outside academia to explain, predict, and improve the behavior of various groups. These range in size from the World Bank and its approaches to development to the composition and compensation of corporate boards, from the inefficiencies of small-town councils to the nuclear aspirations of the ayatollahs of Iran. Bruce Bueno de Mesquita, the preeminent voice behind selectorate theory, has long used his ideas to consult with private corporations, international organizations, and governments. A recently declassified report by the CIA found that, of the intelligence assessments he has made on the agency's behalf (there have been more than a thousand), Bueno de Mesquita has hit the mark twice as often as the CIA's own analysts.[34]

Prospect Theory

It should be clear from the description above that selectorate theory is a *rationalist theory* of political behavior. Drawn from microeconomics, so-called "rational-choice models" rest upon several well-known assumptions: humans are self-interested, possess transitive and complete preferences,[35] and

Aid," *International Organization* 63, no. 2 (Spring 2009): 309–40; Bruce Bueno de Mesquita and Alastair Smith, "Foreign Aid and Policy Concessions," *Journal of Conflict Resolution* 51, no. 2 (April 2007): 251–84.

33. Bruce Bueno de Mesquita, "Leopold II and the Selectorate: An Account in Contrast to a Racial Explanation," *Historical Social Research [Historische Sozialforschung]* 32, no. 4 (2007): 203–21.

34. Clive Thompson, "Can Game Theory Predict When Iran Will Get the Bomb?" *New York Times Magazine*, August 16, 2009, 20.

35. "Transitive" preferences refer to the quality of rationality that means that preferences for one thing over another will remain the same regardless of the order in which these things are introduced. For example, if you prefer A>B and B>C, then you must rationally prefer A>C. "Complete" preferences means that you, *homo economicus*, possess an order of preference for all options that exist. In other words, when faced with any pair of options, you will have a preference for one over the other.

are capable of both pursuing these preferences by connecting strategies with probable outcomes and choosing the strategy that maximizes gain and minimizes loss. In other words, humans know what they want out of all the things they could want, are consistent in these wants, and can figure out the best way to get what they want from all possible ways.

Lesser known, though perhaps of greatest significance, is rational choice theory's dependence upon the assumption of *invariance*. George A. Quattrone and Amos Tversky, two of rational choice's more astute critics, describe it as follows:

> Perhaps the most fundamental principle of rational choice is the assumption of invariance. This assumption, which is rarely stated explicitly, requires that the preference order among prospects should not depend on how their outcomes and probabilities are described and thus that two alternative formulations of the same problem should yield the same choice.[36]

The problem, as one of my students summarized it, is, "We may be rational beings, but we're really just not that good at it." Rational choice theories have been reasonably successful in describing human behavior because these theories rest on assumptions about human nature—specifically, assumptions about egoistic self-interest (or *greed*, if you prefer) that get in touch with the way things really are. That said, rationalist theories tend to ignore the *noetic effects* of the fall—that is, the fall's effects on our minds. Even if human beings want to make decisions based on selfish motivations, it doesn't necessarily follow that

---

36. George A. Quattrone and Amos Tversky, "Contrasting Rational and Psychological Analyses of Political Choice," *The American Political Science Review* 82, no. 3 (September 1988): 727.

we are able to process information such that we reliably do so. In fact, we don't.

Prospect theory emerged in response to observed, predictable patterns of individual decision making that deviated from the expectations of standard, utility-maximizing theories of behavior undergirding traditional microeconomics.[37] Based upon a series of experiments finding that preference is contingent upon the way in which choices are described—contrary to the assumption of invariance—prospect theory holds that individuals respond to gains and losses differently.[38] "Framing" or "formulation effects"—whether a choice is framed in terms of prospective gain or prospective loss—affect the outcome that the individual prefers.[39] The specific ways in which attitudes toward gains and losses differ are twofold:

1. Individuals possess diminishing sensitivities to gains and losses (i.e., the second quarter I find on the sidewalk isn't as exciting as the first, and the third quarter isn't even as exciting as the second); and
2. The negative utility associated with a loss exceeds the positive utility associated with an equivalent gain (i.e., losing twenty dollars hurts more than gaining twenty dollars feels good, even though twenty dollars is twenty dollars).

37. Daniel Kahneman and Amos Tversky, "Prospect Theory: An Analysis of Decision under Risk," *Econometrica* 47, no. 2 (March 1979): 263–92. The description of prospect theory that follows is taken in part from Cale Horne, "Prospect Theory, Social Media and Mobilization for Dissent in Autocracies" (paper presented at the annual meeting of the International Studies Association, San Diego, CA, April 2, 2012).

38. Kahneman and Tversky, "Prospect Theory."

39. Daniel Kahneman and Amos Tversky, "The Psychology of Preferences," *Scientific American* 246, no. 1 (January 1982): 166; Daniel Kahneman and Amos Tversky, "Choices, Values, and Frames," *American Psychologist* 39, no. 4 (April 1984): 346.

These attributes of "variant utility" in decision making are depicted graphically in Fig. 1. By contrast, the invariant function associated with rational choice does not assume a diminishing marginal return or loss, nor does it specify a different functional form for each. As depicted by the diagonal line in Fig. 1, gains and losses are linear and symmetrical in utility, such that expected gains and losses are valued equal to the expectation.

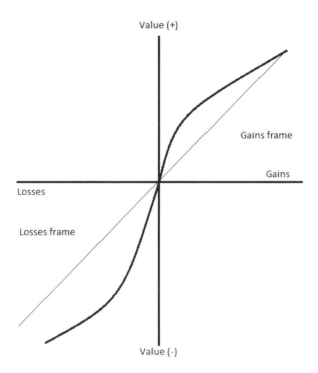

Fig. 1. The framing effect.
The S-shaped, variant utility function is concave with respect to gains and convex with respect to losses. The diagonal line represents the invariant utility function predicted by rational-choice models, where objective gains and losses are assigned a symmetrical subjective value.

Given the variant utilities assumed by prospect theory and observed in experimental settings, it can be said that individuals are *risk averse* with respect to gains and *risk acceptant* with respect to losses. It is the individual's *perception* of the choice, rather than the choice in an objective sense, that determines the individual's attitude toward risk. Perception is dependent on the individual's reference point for choice: the individual is operating in either a "gains frame" or a "losses frame," with attitudes toward risk varying accordingly. Moving from a gains to a losses frame, or vice versa, marks a change in reference point and hence a change in preference.

Such reframing occurs as a matter of changing the individual's perceptions of the choice at hand. Consider, for example, the well-known experiment of Daniel Kahneman (who won a Nobel Prize for prospect theory) and Amos Tversky, in which they confronted a large number of physicians (N = 307) with a fictitious scenario in which they are preparing to respond to a rare Asian disease expected to take the lives of six hundred people.[40] The physicians were presented with one of two choice sets containing objectively identical but differently framed programs of action against the epidemic (see Fig. 2).

In the first choice set, the physicians in the experiment are confronted with a choice between saving two hundred people with certainty (Program A) and the risk of saving or losing all six hundred people (Program B). Subjects faced with this choice consistently chose Program A, preferring the certainty of saving 200 people over the risk of losing everyone. Stated differently, the utility of Program A (U = 200 saved) outweighs the equivalent expected utility of Program B (E(U) = 200 saved).

40. Kahneman and Tversky, "The Psychology of Preferences," 166–67.

Fig. 2. A Kahneman and Tversky framing experiment

Choice Set 1
Program A: 200 people will be saved.
Program B: 1/3 probability that 600 people will be saved; 2/3 probability that no one will be saved.

Choice Set 2
Program C: 400 people will die.
Program D: 1/3 probability that no one will die; 2/3 probability that 600 people will die.

In the second choice set, the utility of Program C is the same as Program A, and the expected utility of Program D is the same as Program B. However, when the choice is framed in terms of prospective loss (i.e., "400 people will die"), the physicians prefer the risk associated with Program D over the certain, negatively framed outcome of Program C.[41] Under conditions of risk aversion, individuals favor the certainty of the status quo over the risk of loss; under conditions of risk acceptance, individuals favor the risk over the certain choice. By contrast, rational choice predicts that individuals will be indifferent in their preference toward any of the four choices, since individuals are modeled as risk neutral and unaffected by perception (i.e., invariant).

In sum, prospect theory offers a model for understanding decision making whereby individuals' perceptions affect choice in a regular, predictable way. As a psychological

---

41. In the original experiment, 72 percent of subjects preferred Program A while only 28 percent of subjects preferred Program B. By contrast, when the choice was reframed, 22 percent of subjects preferred Program C while 78 percent preferred Program D (Kahneman and Tversky, "Choices," 343). For more examples of the experimental effects of the formulation of choices on preferences, see Kahneman and Tversky, "Prospect Theory," and Kahneman and Tversky, "Choices."

model of decision making, prospect theory overcomes the fundamental shortcoming of rational choice theories by assuming that human beings are indeed self-interested, but also that varying decision-making contexts and states of mind mean that we're not necessarily very good at acting on those interests. Prospect theory has been applied fruitfully to empirical puzzles across the discipline: variation in state attitudes of risk aversion and risk acceptance,[42] foreign policy,[43] crisis decision making,[44] war,[45] foreign military intervention,[46] coercive bargaining between states,[47] deterrence and compellence,[48] states' willingness to make and

42. Jeffrey Berejikian, "The Gains Debate: Framing State Choice," *The American Political Science Review* 91, no. 4 (December 1997): 789–805.

43. Rose McDermott, *Risk-Taking in International Politics: Prospect Theory in American Foreign Policy* (Ann Arbor: University of Michigan Press, 1998); Paul A. Kowert and Margaret G. Hermann, "Who Takes Risks? Daring and Caution in Foreign Policy Making," *The Journal of Conflict Resolution* 41, no. 5 (October 1997): 611–37.

44. Barbara Farnham, "Roosevelt and the Munich Crisis: Insights from Prospect Theory," *Political Psychology* 13, no. 2 (June 1992): 205–35; Mark L. Haas, "Prospect Theory and the Cuban Missile Crisis," *International Studies Quarterly* 45, no. 2 (June 2001): 241–70; Rose McDermott, "Prospect Theory in International Relations: The Iranian Hostage Rescue Mission," *Political Psychology* 13, no. 2 (June 1992): 237–63.

45. Rose McDermott and Jacek Kugler, "Comparing Rational Choice and Prospect Theory Analyses: The US Decision to Launch Operation 'Desert Storm,' January 1991," *Journal of Strategic Studies* 24, no. 3 (2001): 49–85; Jack S. Levy, "Loss Aversion, Framing, and Bargaining: The Implications of Prospect Theory for International Conflict," *International Political Science Review / Revue Internationale de Science Politique* 17, no. 2 (April 1996): 179–95.

46. William A. Boettcher III and Michael D. Cobb, "'Don't Let Them Die in Vain': Casualty Frames and Public Tolerance for Escalating Commitment in Iraq," *The Journal of Conflict Resolution* 53, no. 5 (October 2009): 677–97; William A. Boettcher III, "Military Intervention Decisions regarding Humanitarian Crises: Framing Induced Risk Behavior," *The Journal of Conflict Resolution* 48, no. 3 (June 2004): 331–55; Miroslav Nincic, "Loss Aversion and the Domestic Context of Military Intervention," *Political Research Quarterly* 50, no. 1 (March 1997): 97–120.

47. Christopher K. Butler, "Prospect Theory and Coercive Bargaining," *The Journal of Conflict Resolution* 51, no. 2 (April 2007): 227–50.

48. Gary Schaub Jr., "Deterrence, Compellence, and Prospect Theory," *Political Psychology* 25, no. 3 (June 2004): 389–411; Jeffrey D. Berejikian, "A Cognitive Theory of Deterrence," *Journal of Peace Research* 39, no. 2 (March 2002): 165–83.

abide by international agreements,[49] revolution and the problem of collective action,[50] domestic-political coalition building,[51] and economic reform.[52]

The consistent theme of this research is that context affects decision making, making us more fearful or accepting of risky behavior than we might otherwise be—surely something that would-be political practitioners need to know. For example, US Navy line officers may have been a little less forceful in the maritime "quarantine" of Cuba during the Cuban Missile Crisis had they known that Soviet submarine Captain Vitali Grigorievitch Savitsky almost launched his nuclear payload in response to depth charges dropped from American ships. This was coupled with his inability to establish contact with his chain of command and his belief that war had begun—arguably a preference for extreme risk induced by an uncertain, loss-framed environment. In fact, both sides in the conflict moved into a loss frame, which made them more risk acceptant than they should have been, nearly resulting in a nuclear war.[53]

The examples of selectorate theory and prospect theory only scratch the surface of the good work being undertaken in political science today. In terms of research methods,

49. Jeffrey D. Berejikian, *International Relations under Risk: Framing State Choice* (Albany: SUNY Press, 2004).

50. Jeffrey Berejikian, "Revolutionary Collective Action and the Agent-Structure Problem," *The American Political Science Review* 86, no. 3 (September 1992): 647–57; Daniel Masters, "Support and Nonsupport for Nationalist Rebellion: A Prospect Theory Approach," *Political Psychology* 25, no. 5 (October 2004): 703–26.

51. Maria Fanis, "Collective Action Meets Prospect Theory: An Application to Coalition Building in Chile, 1973–75," *Political Psychology* 25, no. 3 (June 2004): 363–88.

52. Kurt Weyland, "The Political Fate of Market Reform in Latin America, Africa, and Eastern Europe," *International Studies Quarterly* 42, no. 4 (December 1998): 645–73; Kurt Weyland, "Risk Taking in Latin American Economic Restructuring: Lessons from Prospect Theory," *International Studies Quarterly* 40, no. 2 (June 1996): 185–207.

53. Haas, "Prospect Theory and the Cuban Missile Crisis," 253–66.

these and other areas of research are explored using natural and laboratory experiments, qualitative methods such as process tracing and most-similar/most-different system designs, frequentist and Bayesian statistical modeling, and non-statistical quantitative methods like computational network analysis. Frequently these methods are used in conjunction with one another and, when properly employed, can provide us with new understandings of the political world and the *homo politicus* who inhabits that world.

CONCLUSION: "DR. HORNE, I THINK I'M INTERESTED IN GOING INTO POLITICS . . ."

I regularly hear these words from students considering studies in political science or a related field. This is an exciting thing for a college professor! It is personally gratifying to see capable, earnest students go into vocations that my discipline most directly speaks to and for which it can best prepare them: careers in government, inter- or non-governmental organizations (IGOs and NGOs), the military, and journalism, to name a few. Government professionals are well served to understand the different theories aimed at explaining institutional success and failure and the methods available to measure them. NGOs' strategies for poverty alleviation or conflict resolution will be greatly affected by how well the organization's leaders understand the nature of the collective-action problems that prevent people from cooperating even when it is in their mutual interest to do so. Military leaders will offer very different policy advice, and will take very different strategic postures, based on their particular understanding of the psychological under-pinnings of deterrence theory. Journalists will pen quite different stories about congressional gridlock if they grasp the core insights of selectorate theory and how the logic of leadership survival interacts with political institutions. If the reader is convinced, as I am, that our fundamental beliefs about the world—and indeed our fundamental relationship with that world's Creator and Sustainer—matter for how we interpret the world, then surely we want faithful, learned Christians to be engaged in these things.

That said, I also want to help these students think carefully about what it means to be a follower of Christ in the arena of politics, moving beyond vague admonitions of "winning culture for Christ," "redeeming fallen society," and the like. These slogans may ultimately prove discouraging and spiritually harmful when the student doesn't see tangible evidence of institutional or societal change after a few years' work in Washington, DC.

I urge the reader who is interested in "going into politics" or a related career to consider the context of Matthew 5:45, which is often used to illustrate the idea of common grace but is almost always taken out of context (as it was above when I quoted it!). Recall the statement: "[God] makes his sun rise on the evil and on the good, and sends rain on the just and on the unjust." In the context of Jesus' words in the Sermon on the Mount, though, the text is about *loving one's enemies.* God does not simply give the gifts of sun and rain as if that's the end of the story. Rather, we as God's children are to pattern our behavior after his gracious precedent, loving our enemies "that [we] may be sons of [our] Father who is in heaven" (v. 45). In other words, our heavenly identity as sons of God is borne out in our interactions in the world, even (perhaps especially) with the unbelieving world. "If you love those who love you, what reward do you have? Do not even the tax collectors do the same? And if you greet only your brothers, what more are you doing than others? Do not even the Gentiles do the same?" (v. 46–47).

In this sense, God's people are not merely beneficiaries of God's common grace to the world—the blessings of sun and rain given to the just and unjust alike—but also active participants in the dispensing of this grace. Rather than our retreating from the world, our engagement with it—including participation in the academic disciplines and other human institutions—is an act of love patterned after God's love of his creation, even in its fallen state. And this loving engagement with the world is not an end in itself, but is part of the church's role in the unfolding plan of God, as we look forward to the consummation of all things when Christ comes again. Paradoxically, we love God's enemies because we love God and anticipate our perfected, heavenly union with him. This is how Jesus concludes his discourse on love of enemies in the text: "You therefore must be perfect, as your heavenly Father is perfect" (v. 48).

By engaging in the academic disciplines, we are loving our enemies. We begin with antithesis, mindful that God is Creator and interpreter of all reality, and then we enter confidently into the realm of common grace, where our enemies (who due to unbelief have declared themselves enemies of God) are paradoxically engaged with us in the mysterious unfolding of creation. We genuinely acknowledge the contributions of unbelievers in this development—which, in the case of academia, usually dwarf the tangible contributions made by believers—and we are blessed by them. Such a view stands in stark contrast with Christians who dismiss political science, advancing a "politics according to the Bible" argument that trivializes both God's general and special revelation. We cannot know exactly how every scholarly finding advances the unfolding of creation and the progressive differentiation of the lines of Seth and Cain, but we rest secure in the knowledge that these developments are purposeful in a final, eschatological sense.

DISCUSSION QUESTIONS

1. The author argues that, "regardless of one's theology or place on the ideological spectrum, there is a baptized political movement to match." Think about your own church experiences. What contemporary political positions have you heard argued from pulpits, with a scriptural backing claimed for them? What do you think of how Scripture was used to make the preacher's point? How might that same passage be connected to the Bible's overarching message of the gospel?

2. What do you think of the idea of common grace, in both its constant and progressive senses? How might this idea affect where we get our news, what our attitudes are toward expertise in various fields, or how we vote? What does the author mean by the admonition that antithesis must precede common grace?

3. Think of a recent event that you have heard explained through vague appeals to culture: "That's just their culture," "That's just the way those people are," etc. How might an understanding of both group and elite interests, formal and informal institutions, and the competing interests of other groups and elites offer a more full-fledged explanation of the event?

4. Consider the case of contemporary Nigeria. Presently the largest economy in Africa, Nigeria has immense oil wealth and economic potential yet is plagued by crippling corruption, with nearly three-quarters of the population living in poverty. Further, the country's modern military is seemingly unable to defeat a relatively lightly equipped jihadist militia, Boko Haram, operating in the country's north. How can selectorate theory help us to understand the glaring disconnect between state resources and state performance?

5. Consider the following scenario between two fictitious world powers. State A enters into a series of free-trade treaties and mutual-defense pacts with a group of smaller countries surrounding another world power, State B. State B responds by extending its claims of sovereignty in the surrounding seas and militarily occupying a series of disputed islands also claimed by its less powerful neighbors. State A responds by conducting joint naval exercises in the region with its new trading partners, including maneuvers through disputed waters and flyovers of the disputed islands. State B responds with a series of medium- and long-range missile tests and marine-landing exercises, even positioning several submarines in proximity to State A's naval exercise. Can prospect theory help us to predict the missteps that both powers are susceptible to committing?

6. What would you say to the college-bound high school senior intent on a political career in Washington, DC? What encouragements and warnings would you offer? Or, if you yourself are such a high school senior, what encouragements and warnings would you expect to hear or hope to hear?

SERIES AFTERWORD

Christians are called to enter, engage, and cultivate every sphere of lawful human activity. And increasingly, in our modern age, this calling requires us to receive training in specialized disciplines beyond the high school level. We must enter colleges, universities, and technical schools to develop knowledge and skills that will equip us to engage in good, even necessary cultural activities in the humanities, the sciences, technology, and the fine arts. But many

Christian families are justifiably anxious about sending their children into the modern secular academy to obtain such training; many assume that the norms and beliefs under which the modern academic disciplines operate are at odds with the values their children have been taught in their homes and churches.

While it is important for Christians to instill in one another a biblical framework—a "Christian worldview"— that will help us to understand and interpret what we learn in faithful ways, it is also necessary to consider the fact that the modern academic disciplines are good gifts from a good and gracious God. And they are each packed with insights—"common grace insights"—that can and should be used for the good of the world and the glory of God.

Faithful Learning is a series of modest-sized booklets that provide Christian invitations to the modern academic disciplines. Each volume will introduce students—along with teachers and other educational professionals—to a distinct academic discipline and will challenge readers to grapple with the foundational ideas, practices, and applications found in each of them. The authors of these booklets are highly trained Christian scholars who operate under the assumption that, when understood rightly, each of their disciplines holds the potential for students to cultivate a deeper love for God and for their neighbors. It is our hope and prayer that these booklets will be used by Christians to engage their academic studies with greater confidence and understanding, and that they will thereby be more equipped to *learn faithfully* about whatever pursuit or sphere of human activity God is calling them to.

Jay D. Green

MORE ON FAITHFUL LEARNING
IN ACADEMIC STUDIES

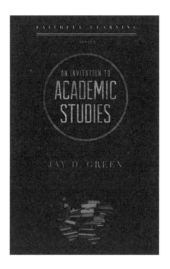

"We were not wrong to learn the alphabet just because they say that the god Mercury was its patron, nor should we avoid justice and virtue just because they dedicated temples to justice and virtue. . . . A person who is a good and a true Christian should realize that truth belongs to his Lord, wherever it is found."
—Augustine, *On Christian Doctrine*

Why study academic disciplines like history, literature, biology, philosophy, chemistry, and computer science? Why even study secular subjects in the first place—especially since we have the Bible to learn from? God has made us to be nonstop learners—and what we learn can actually strengthen our faith! What will *you* learn, and why?

Jay Green invites you to explore the world of academic study, where you will discover vital opportunities to understand and expand God's kingdom. Learn how the church and the academy intersect, and find out how you can cultivate your mind for the glory of God.

MORE FROM P&R ON POLITICAL STUDIES

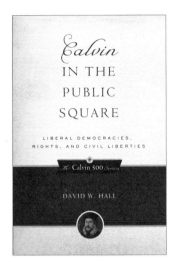

David Hall explores John Calvin's extraordinary influence on what we consider the key elements of a modern, compassionate, and just society—particularly the fields of liberal democracy, rights, and civil liberties.

"What a fantastic book that presents a great historical and theological overview of Calvinism regarding government. Hall shows how this theology of government reform works beyond Calvin and the Reformers and eventually becomes the foundational fabric of colonial America."
—Rob Fields, Congressional and Legislators Fellowship Groups

"Hall presents a very well researched account of Calvin's thoughts on important political ideas. He provides insights and a historical account of Calvin's influence that is relevant for both the church and political thinkers today."
—David Gray, Workforce and Family Program, New America Foundation, Washington, D.C.

Politics has become something of a joke—but not a funny one.

Sound bites and knee-jerk reactions have replaced reasoned debate, and the church appears to wear a one-size-fits-all political jacket. Isn't it time to think a bit deeper?

Carl Trueman takes you on a readable, provocative, and lively romp through Christianity and politics.

"Our political choices are very often between relative goods and lesser evils. *Republocrat* is the honest and heartfelt lament of a talented theologian's struggle with the limited choices before us. Well argued, and well worth arguing with, Trueman's book has the potential to spark lively conversations and much needed debate. Let's hope so." —Michael Cromartie, former Commissioner of the United States Commission on International Religious Freedom